Return to Melita

Two Weeks in Malta, a Travelogue,

and a Memoir

Anne Fiorentino Pflug

Return to Melita
Copyright © 2017 Anne Fiorentino Pflug
ISBN: 978-0-9986953-7-2
  Library of Congress Control Number: 2018903098

Front cover: Fort St. Elmo, a star fort, stands on the peninsula that divides the Grand Harbor. It protects the approach to the main harbor of Malta. Best known for its roles in the Great Siege of Malta of 1566 as well as in World War II.   Photo by Anne Pflug

Back cover: The medieval city of Mdina stands as a sentinel in the Maltese countryside. It was originally Malta's capital when the Knights of St. John arrived in Malta around 1500. Sometimes called the Silent City.
                      Photo by Anne Pflug

La Maison Publishing, Inc.
Vero Beach Florida
The Hibiscus City
lamaisonpublishing@gmail.com

For my late husband, George,

Who never made it to Malta with me.

A special Thank You to my good friend and author, Margie Miklas, without whose encouragement and support this book would never have seen the light of day.

Preface

Whenever I am introduced, whether socially or professionally, I am usually asked where I come from. I have an accent but it is hard to identify and when I respond that I come from Malta, I usually receive a quizzical look. Where is Malta?? Is that Italian??

I usually respond that no, it is not Italian although we are very close to Italy.

Usually then, I mention some anecdote in my life that happened in Malta and the response usually is: "Wow, you should write a book about it!"

Well, I decided that I would, and the following is a compilation of several vacations that I took, not always with the same company but always happy to be back in the land of my birth and proud to show Malta off to whomever, be it my children, friends or family that had not been there.

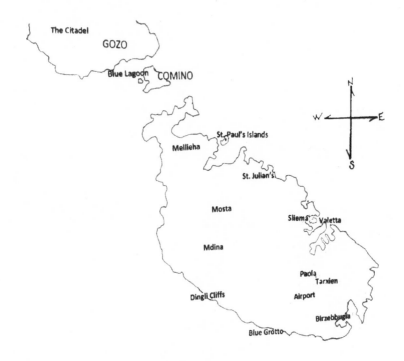

Malta

Melita is the personification of Malta. Originally, it was the name of the ancient capital city, Melite, named by the Romans, which eventually became Mdina.

Table of Contents

Background information about Malta

As a child, I lived on the island of Malta. It was the whole world to me and imagine my surprise when, as I got older, I discovered that the island of Malta was just a small dot on most maps, if it appeared at all.

I spent the first ten years of my life in Malta and, as a child, learned a great deal about its history. The Maltese have a great deal to be proud of. Their little island country was extremely important in many historical events – starting from being mentioned in *Homer's* Odyssey, being the landing place where St. Paul was shipwrecked on his way to Rome, participating in The Great Siege in the Middle Ages as well as being an important

British *Fortress* during World War Two. Originally, the Romans named its capital city, Melite which later became Mdina and the name Melite eventually turned into Malta, the present name for the whole country.

As anyone who reads about it can discover, Malta has an ancient and glorious history. Officially, Malta is the largest of three islands, which make up the Maltese archipelago. It is dead center in the Mediterranean Sea. So much so that in most atlases, which present a two-page spread of that sea, Malta ends up being in the center, between the two pages, sometimes not seen at all.

Malta is south of Italy and north of Libya. It is 17 miles (27 km) long and 9 miles (14.5

kilometers) wide, for a total of 153 square miles (391.5 square kilometers). In the perspective of where most of us live, I sometimes traveled 20 or so miles to go shopping, or to the doctor's, a distance which extends beyond Malta's length. Again, my childhood perspective was such that Malta seemed very large to me.

Maltese people, including my family when I lived in Malta, actually had a summer place on the water to which we traveled for vacations all the way from inland which had to be just a few miles. In my recent visits to Malta I found this to be strange! I am now in the final planning stage of my bi-annual trip to Malta and am always amazed at the changes that become obvious every time I arrive.

I remember that when I was a child, Malta was governed by the British although the most important influence was the Catholic Church. This religion, which was introduced to the island by St. Paul after his shipwreck there, had very strict and controlling rules by which we lived. So much so that I can still remember, when the circus came to the island, the performers had to get special permission from the Bishop to wear two-piece costumes. On my last visit, I was witness to topless sunbathing in some of the most prestigious hotels. I have, therefore, a twofold perspective when it comes to seeing Malta.

Because traveling to Europe from the United States is a long journey to start with, I always try to combine my trip to Malta with a visit to another country. I have come to Malta via Amsterdam, Rome and the Amalfi coast as well as from Sicily. This time, we arrived in Malta from Nuremberg, via Frankfurt. Malta is accessible from all over Europe and, to the Europeans, especially northern Europeans, it is a place to vacation. They think of it similarly, to how we consider the Caribbean. Malta is not reached from the States in one flight but, if you can get to the major cities of Europe, you can get to Malta.

Anne Pflug

Day 1 – Saturday, Arriving in Malta

The first view of Malta, in the summer, is not too beautiful. Summer is the dry season and all you see from the plane is a brown, rocky landscape. Greenery is reserved for the winter. What was beautiful to me was the happy, smiling faces of my family.

Upon leaving the plane, we were welcomed by my cousins, Joe, Liz, his wife and Diana her sister. Joe and Liz had been to the states, that past May and I was eager to see them again.

Like the entire world, it seems, this summer of 2015 was extremely hot and Malta was no different. We could feel the heat immediately when we opened the doors from the plane to the outside. It wasn't any hotter than the Florida heat we had left behind in the States but, with the brown landscape and no trees in bloom, it just seemed less inviting.

We decided to break our time in Malta into two parts. The first part, we stayed in Sliema, a very busy city catering especially to tourists. You hear multiple languages here and the hotel personnel as well as restauranteurs and other vendors usually speak several languages.

Malta's official languages are Maltese and English, Maltese historically and English through the gentle occupation of Malta during the time before independence.

***

My cousins dropped us off at the Preluna Hotel in Sliema and we were very impressed.

We have been to some beautiful hotels as well as some not so beautiful in Malta and here, we were met with a welcome drink and a lot of happy smiles as we registered for our stay. We unpacked a bit, looked around, and then started off to explore the area. One of the better amenities in this hotel was the

Penthouse Lounge, which was a rooftop lounge with a great view of the area including all of Sliema and other parts nearby from a 13th floor perch. We immediately made plans to go up in the evening for a drink and entertainment. Later, we went for a walk along the Sliema Promenade, a lovely walk, though crowded with tourists, and eventually we stopped at a seaside restaurant for a Maltese dinner at The Fortizza. Dinner was Fenech (rabbit), a Maltese specialty, and it was delicious. I had not had rabbit since I was a child and thoroughly enjoyed the childhood memories that came to me as I ate. As we were returning to our room, in the elevator, we met a Maltese lady who was visiting Malta after 60 years away. She presently lived in

Australia, one of the countries that has a large number of Maltese and was as totally amazed as I had been, at the changes she saw in Malta.

Because we were a bit tired, having had to get up very early for our flight from Nuremberg to Frankfurt, we decided to retire early. We did however, spend a bit of time in the Penthouse Lounge. Malta, at night, all lit up, is even more beautiful than it was in the daytime. We had a wonderful time there.

We danced a bit, snacked with our drinks and listened to an entertaining lady singing popular songs. I find it amazing, and proof of our very small world, that here, on the island of Malta, the music was exactly the same as we have in the States. We had a lovely time; it was a beautiful ending to our first day!

11

My cousin Joe had given us an itinerary for our stay in Malta. He is recently retired so he offered to chauffer us around for part of this trip. A wonderful perc for us! But, as I usually do when I visit a foreign country or a new city, I book my first few days on the Hop On Hop Off city tour. Malta is a very small island as compared to many international cities, and each part of the sightseeing tour with this company actually took us to half of the island. We planned to take both tours, the North part of Malta and the South part of Malta. Each tour, if you don't get off at any stop, takes approximately half a day. As we did plan to make a few stops, we allowed ourselves two days for these two tours. To me, it was well worth it to take these tours as to do so gave me a good review of what I wanted to explore and see and introduce to my 'first time ever in Malta' friend, Bob. These tours give me the 'lay of the land', so to speak. After these tours, we were ready to go back to places we liked, to see them in more detail and absorb them in more depth.

And then, we planned, with the help of my cousin, Joe, to go to the places he picked for us to see. In this way, we got to see Malta as tourists and then, to see it as a native would show it. We had the best of both worlds!

Day 2 – Sunday, the Southern Route

For our first full day in Malta, we had a light breakfast at the hotel and, since it was Sunday, made plans to go to Mass. We took a cab to the Millennium Chapel, less than twenty minutes away. The chapel was in St. Julian's Bay and I was familiar with it from previous trips. It was a beautiful chapel, modern and unlike the usual Maltese churches which are usually very Gothic in style. It seems to have been built for tourists and is surrounded by the Hilton and near the Radisson Hotel.

The mass was in Maltese but halfway through, the priest switched to English. I assume it was because he saw many visitors to the island in attendance. Although I understand a great deal of the language, I could not understand the priest. I did sing the hymns and say the prayers in Maltese. It seemed that I could understand the written word much better than the spoken word. They speak so fast!

After Mass, we strolled around in the area, snacked on some pastizzi and enjoyed a leisurely Sunday morning, before we headed back to our hotel to start our day.

Generally, the various tour companies make it very easy for tourists to travel all over Malta. Besides the excellent transportation system, which is very easy to use, the tour companies go out of their way to pick up tourists at their hotel and bring them to the tour starting point. It was actually very easy to take the bus from Sliema to Valletta, to the Waterfront Terminus but, since the company offered us a ride right from our hotel, we took that.

***

Now we were ready for the first part of our tour. Since the Hop On Hop Off busses circle the island, we could get on anywhere, but we did choose to get on in Valletta, which made an excellent starting point.

The busses are two decker and equipped with information about what we're seeing in five languages. Because we anticipated a really hot day, we chose to sit on the bottom deck, inside. It was a bit more comfortable and we wanted to see how this first part of the tour went. Our first stop was Tarxien with its Temples and the Hypogeum. We were sure that we were going to come back here so we did not get off at this time.

The next stop was one of the Three Cities, Vittoriosa and we did stop and get off here. We visited the Maritime Museum which is housed in an old Naval Bakery built by the British Military in the 19th Century. Because

Vittoriosa, as well as the other two cities are located on the Grand Harbor, they all have wonderful marinas with many large and fancy yachts. We enjoyed walking around here for a while before we continued on. Following a tour of the Three Cities, our bus headed to the fishing village of Marsaxlokk. It was pleasant to get off here and walk around and admire the traditionally painted fishing boats, all with eyes painted on the prow, tied to their moorings in one of Malta's main fishing village. Historically, these painted eyes are part of an ages old superstition which says that the eyes protect the fisherman when the waters are wild.

These tour busses are very prompt and another one comes along about every 45 minutes, so we learned to take our time and walk around, stop for a drink and possibly shop in the open market, set up especially for the tourists. There are also numerous restaurants in the area. Marsaxlokk is on another beautiful bay, this time a fishing bay as opposed to the boating and tourist facilities we saw in Sliema and Vittoriosa. No yachts here. Then, we headed for the southwestern part, an area very lightly inhabited and, at this time of year, very arid and dry looking. The area is also very steep with the bus going up and down the hills. Our destination here was the Blue Grotto, a picturesque area where the crystal-clear waters seemed to reflect the colorful fluorescent underwater. I knew we were planning to return here with Joe so we did not get off but did enjoy the breezes that came from the Mediterranean Sea at this time of day. Very close to the Blue Grotto are some of the most impressive prehistoric temples, the ones called Hagar Qim and Mnajdra. Unfortunately, we had to choose which of the prehistoric temples we would visit on this trip and these were not the ones we chose. I know I will return and I definitely will visit these two at another time.

***

It is amazing and hard for me to understand how traveling a few miles on such a small island takes so much time. The morning, and part of the afternoon, already gone, we are now again heading for Valletta, a bit of touring and a nice lunch at one of the outdoor restaurants circling the city. Since we had traveled over half the island in one day and had seen all things Maltese, we felt a bit nostalgic about home and decided to have a late lunch at the Hard Rock Café. This restaurant was perfect for enjoying a couple of cool drinks and indulging in some delicious, comfortable, and familiar foods. Bob had yummy ribs while I had a fantastic hamburger. The staff was great, very welcoming and terrific with their suggestions. And, since many restaurants here do not have air conditioning, it was a welcome bonus to dine, not in the middle of the very crowded city but on the waterfront, where the Mediterranean breezes always blow. We had an opportunity to unwind, relax and enjoy the area. And, since at that time, I was collecting Hard Rock Café sweatshirts, I added to my collection with a Malta sweatshirt. We plan to spend a complete day in Valletta later and, as I had already mentioned, this day was simply to reacquaint me with this beautiful island and solidify the plans to visit some areas in more depth later.

After we ended our tour of *The Southern Route*, we decided to enjoy a bit more of Valletta considering the weather was becoming more agreeable, and not too hot. Even with two full days here, we could not see all there was to see in Valletta. We made several quick stops including the War Museum and Fort St. Elmo. The War Museum itself is located within the precincts of Fort St. Elmo. It is packed with loads of militaria from the British Period and it contains a pictorial documentary of the Second World War. Included in the exhibits is the most important George Cross, awarded to the Maltese people by King George for their valor and courage in the war.

Cruise ship passengers and visitors coming to Malta by boat get their first glimpse of the island as they enter the Grand Harbor and see Fort St. Elmo. The fort is situated at the tip of Valletta and has, for centuries, been the major defense of the two harbors. Such defense was best documented in books about the Great Siege of 1565 when Malta was invaded by the Saracens in their attempt to conquer Europe in the Middle Ages and again during World War II when Malta was the only Allied defense against the surrounding Axis in the Mediterranean. It is well worth seeing this fort on certain Sundays when special re-enactments take place. We were fortunate to arrive at such a time. The historically authentic costumes in vibrant colors, the cannons going off and the smoke created by them made the performance a feast for all the senses. It was a great touring end to our first day in Malta. We took public transportation to our home away from home and later, at our hotel, we had a late dinner and enjoyed the view of Malta from the Penthouse Lounge. We turned in early as our first day of exploration of Malta was exciting but very tiring. We will build stamina as we go further into our time here.

Tomorrow we will again board the Hop On Hop Off bus. This time we will do *The Northern Route* where we will see a different part of Malta and another harbor, with a completely different history, St. Paul's Bay.

Day 3 – Monday, the Northern Route

This time by taking the *Northern Route* on the Hop On Hop Off busses, we will be going to a mostly unfamiliar area for me, as this is not anywhere that I traveled to as a child. Since we were staying in Sliema, at the Preluna Hotel, we were conveniently picked up there. This is actually stop 16 but, as the tour goes in a continuous circle, we will end up here and will have seen all of northern Malta. The first stop was the Sliema Ferries. We made note of this as we plan to do a Harbor Cruise later this week so we did not get off. The next stop, where we did get off for a short visit was another section of Valletta, at the Phoenicia Hotel and the Main Gate. All tours seem to pass through Valletta, as it is the original starting and ending point for both. The Main Gate is presently under construction as it was decided that it had to be modernized. I personally did not like this plan because I had fond memories of the time when I was a child and the Main gate and the Phoenicia Hotel were reliable standbys at the entrance of the Capital City. By modernizing this area, I felt that they were changing a part of Malta's history. This gate was a gigantic stone construction and, I imagine, in medieval times, it closed its giant doors at the end of the day for the safety of the residents. We were able to climb the steps to the bastions, the larger of which is St. Andrew's Bastion. It gives one a good view of the Bus Terminal, which surrounds a beautiful, sculptured fountain. The Phoenicia Hotel, the Cathedral in Floriana and the distant landscape are also in view from this bastion. While here, I made sure to take some photos of the Floriana Cathedral. I wanted to compare it to a photo that I had taken in 1950. The bastion was a perfect place from which to photograph and I managed to get just about the same view, so many years later. We entered the Gate and were confronted by a mass of people. Cars do not use the main roads in Valletta too often and the people walk all over. When a car does need to use the roads, the driver honks his horn and the people separate, for the moment, and let him pass.

One of my favorite corners, close to the entrance came into full view. It was Wembley's, a drug store/ice cream store. Again, the memories of my childhood had me getting ice cream here over 65 years ago! And it still looked the same inside, dark, narrow aisles and crowded, although I did not remember the products offered at that time, except for the ice cream. We continued strolling down the main street, Republic Street which starts from the City Gate and goes straight down to Fort St. Elmo and the harbor. Here was a perfect opportunity to enjoy an ice cream cone. As I remembered from so long ago, it was still refreshing and delicious. The weather was perfect for it, hot! And, it made strolling on this street much more pleasurable.

***

I would consider one of the best first stops in Valletta to be The Malta Experience located on St. Elmo's Bastion. It is an audio-visual spectacle that gives the observer a wonderful introduction to the history and achievements of the Maltese Islands. Malta, in the center of the Mediterranean, has always been buffeted by world events; the bravery of the Maltese has been tested often and they have shown to be a strong and resilient people. This program clearly shows such achievements. I recommend it highly to a new visitor to the island.

The commentary covers 7000 years of history including insights into the early settlers of the temple period, through the Great Siege with the Knights of Malta and including Malta's important activities during World War II.

Considering Malta is such a small island, and Valletta smaller still, we found a great many areas to explore in the city and we know we will be back here to spend a complete day later in the week. At this time, we did stop at a nice craft shop and saw quite a few souvenirs that we knew we would pick up later, on our next excursion into Valletta.

For the time being, we got back on the Hop On Hop Off bus and headed off to San Anton Gardens. These are just beautiful, peaceful areas where one can relax and enjoy the calm, quiet atmosphere, especially after having been in very crowded and busy Valletta. Originally, this was San Anton Palace and Garden and it served as a beautiful green oasis in the middle of the much built up area of Attard and Balzan.

The palace had served as the residence of the Grand Master Antoine de Paule as well as a residence of the British Governors. The Palace now also houses The Corinthian Room Restaurant in which we dined, later in the week. Top chefs have created exquisite dishes for Royalty in these kitchens and it was a pleasure dining in the same environment as they. Service, offering an international menu, is discreet and impeccable with a touch of class. We continued on to Mdina but we did not get off here. We had plans to spend a whole day here with my cousins later in the week. On the way to Mdina, we stopped at another beautifully set up Craft Village where we were able to purchase blown glass vases and handmade lace as well as a variety of other crafts. Then we drove by the Mosta Church but, again, did not stop here today.

Our next major village to visit was Bugibba, essentially a summer resort although there are Maltese living here year-round.

There are many hotels, restaurants and fun places to visit and since this is situated on a mini peninsula next to St. Paul's Bay, the enticing view of the Mediterranean Sea is all around. After enjoying lunch outdoors in the pleasant salty air of the area, we were ready to start heading for 'home'. It was a long day but we enjoyed every minute of it. On the way, we passed the Westin Dragonara with its sumptuous Casino as well as the Hilton Malta in St. Julian's. Both hotels are worth visiting and are definitely a pleasure to stay in.

Having finished the northern circle, we were dropped off at our hotel so that we could relax and have a drink before dinner.

***

We decided on a 'close by' dinner tonight. We were a bit tired from all that sightseeing, even though we were on busses throughout the day. Dinner tonight was in Sliema, a nice walk from our hotel. Tigne Point, where the restaurant is located, is a resort complex and the restaurant itself gives one a magnificent view of Malta's baroque capital across the creek. The restaurant itself, La Cucina Del Sole was quite a nice restaurant whose offerings can be defined by the 3 P's, Pizza, Pasta and Pesce. We chose the pizza; it had been a while since we had one and their choices were terrific. We chose the Mediterranean Pizza which, besides the basics included marinated octopus and local red prawns. You've got to be adventurous sometimes! In addition, we included the whole Buffalo Mozzarella, which was awesome! Returning, we planned to take the bus. It was a very short ride to our hotel so we lingered, enjoying the view until it was late, and we were tired and ready for a goodnight's sleep.

Tomorrow we plan to visit Mdina, the Silent City as well as other points in Malta. The weather was great for our first few days, although quite a bit hot. I hoped it will continue to be sunny and beautiful.

Day 4 – Tuesday, Mdina and Blue Grotto

Today we had a really full day. The weather was perfect and we decided to make the most of it. Joe picked us up at 9:30 and proceeded to take us all over the island. Our first stop was the church in Mosta, nearby where Joe and his family lived.

Mosta is most famous for its dome, the Rotunda of the Church of the Assumption. It is a parish church built between 1833 and 1860 in an impressive neo-classic style said to be inspired by the Pantheon in Rome. The dome is the third largest unsupported dome in the world! It is, however, most famous for the fact that during World War II, a bomb fell through the dome and did not explode. It lay on the large circular floor of the church until it was detonated. I still remember hearing about this bomb and how the ever-superstitious Maltese were sure that it was a miracle and a foreshadowing of the victory that, we felt at the time, Malta was important in achieving. Upon entering the church, you can see the patched-up hole in the dome and, as you proceed to the sacristy, you can take a photograph with the now safe, neutralized bomb. We also took photographs in front of the beautifully designed church.

It is interesting to note that upon entering the church I had to be 'loaned' a large scarf to cover my shoulders because I was not wearing sleeves. This is very typical of all churches in Europe. It happened to me at the Vatican in Rome as well as in Cologne Cathedral in Germany.

After Mosta, Joe drove us to Mdina. Mosta seemed to us to be a commercial center and lacked the charm of the small surrounding villages. Other than the most famous dome, we found nothing more of interest here. I had been there before, but it was new to my accompanying friend.

***

L'Imdina was the old capital city of Malta, the one that was originally titled Melite by the Romans. It became known as the Silent City and its official designation is Citta Notabile. This city is characterized by Medieval as well as Baroque architecture and here, it seems as if time has stood still.

Mdina traces its history to a time earlier than when St. Paul the Apostle was shipwrecked in Malta and was said to have lived in this area.

Mdina is called the Silent City because the great and thick walls invite quiet. The walls are as thick as some rooms, more than 10 feet thick in some areas. It has always been the home to Maltese noble families, with their impressive palaces and typically narrow streets and was the capital when the Knights of St. John arrived in Malta around 1500. Descendants of these lucky people still reside in Mdina and these are the only ones with permission to drive through its very historic streets.

The 12th century Roman Catholic St. Paul's Cathedral dominates the main square and characterizes the city with its unique skyline. An earthquake destroyed the original church in 1693 and the present church was built in its place. From the city's bastions, one can enjoy a panoramic view of Malta's north and eastern countryside.

A lovely and very popular outdoor restaurant, The Fontanella, occupies one of the bastions where one can enjoy the famous Maltese pastizzi. A delight!!

Another restaurant, the very upscale Bacchus is also outdoors and has elaborate canopies to shield diners from the hot sun. It can even be enjoyed in the evening, when the rest of Mdina itself is closed to tourists.

We did stop at the Fontinella, the restaurant on the bastions and enjoyed the ever popular pastizzi with beer for lunch. We took a lot of photos and enjoyed the fantastic view from these heights. We walked around the whole city discovering narrow roads and small chapels and even small apartments.

Typical of Medieval architecture, the city was surrounded by a moat, now dry and turned into a low-level park and including, of course, a gift shop. We bought some beautiful glass and lace, souvenirs of the Silent City.

After we exited through the Main Gate, the same gate that can still be closed at dusk, we spent the rest of the afternoon along the greenway, in the town of Rabat, an area that was crowded with tourists, buses, the ever popular carozzin and people watchers of many nationalities. We, too, enjoyed walking around and watching the crowds. We took photos around the carozzins, the horse drawn carriages set up specifically for the tourists and supplying transportation typical of all important places around the world. I'm sure we missed some areas of Mdina; it is not only silent but also mysterious, but all in all, we felt we saw a great deal of this ancient city which still reminds one of the Middle Ages.

Mdina ceased to be the capital in 1530 when the honor was given to Birgu, Citta Vittoriosa, with a population of 300. Vittoriosa had been the capital city under the Knights of Malta between 1530 and 1571. Presently it has a population of 2700.

***

Throughout our ride, heading home, we saw many stone walls and winding country roads. There were loads of 'Bajtar tax Xewk' cactus growing wild. I remember that, as a child, I enjoyed traveling, with my family, these same roads on a donkey cart, eating this wild fruit, prickly pears, and having a wonderful time. We had to be careful picking the fruit as it was covered with thorns but it was delicious and well worth the caution. Sometimes I even find prickly pears available in the states and eating them always brings back fond memories of my childhood in Malta.

Later, we stopped for an early dinner in Sliema at one of the beachfront restaurants. We chose the Surfside Bar and Grill because it was close and had such good reviews. We were looking for casual ambience, which we found here. It's an open-air restaurant under roof so that we could enjoy being outside and yet not be in the hot sun. The restaurant gave us a fantastic panoramic view of the sea as we watched the waves splash against the rocks. And, most important, the food was delicious with good size portions. You do develop quite an appetite when you're exploring all day!

Here, in Sliema, one does not see the authentic buildings and the many churches that are found throughout the island. Sliema has become a large tourist city. There is a continuous vision of cranes, cement trucks and other construction vehicles all over the place. New condos are rising throughout the area. It was explained to me that just recently, new construction rules permit buildings to be built higher than was previously allowed. As a result, there has erupted a renaissance of buildings, hotels and other tourist homes in the area. After dinner, touring with my cousin again, we revisited the small village of Rabat on our way to the Blue Grotto, a diving and touristy area on the west coast of Malta. This was our second and longer visit here. We were able to buy tickets to go on a short boat ride to see the beautiful grotto with fluorescent light under water. In addition, we saw many divers taking advantage of the beautiful, clear waters to explore this phenomenon at close range. Since it was an unusually hot week, we stopped for a cold drink and had facetime with my family in Florida. It's worth noting that wherever we went, we found Wi-Fi to be available and free. Who knew? This island, barely known by the modern world and just recently discovered by American tourists, would be so up to date in computer devices.

As we continued driving in this area, we could get a view of Filfla, an uninhabited rock that sometimes is considered another island adding to the Maltese archipelago. It is a large, rectangular, solid island seemingly floating in the Mediterranean.

It was getting late, and we did have a full day, so Joe drove us back to our hotel in Sliema to enjoy a much-needed rest, an ice cream cone and a pleasant promenade around the tourist filled coast of Sliema.

Day 5 – Wednesday, Bir Zebbugia, Tarxien

Because Malta is not such a large place, it was no effort to head back to the last spot we visited to continue our 'tour' of Malta.

As we were on the southern coast, we passed through Zurrieq on our way to Marsaxlokk, another lovely quaint fishing village on the coast. We enjoyed strolling

along the water here as well as looking
through the various touristy offerings
available all around us. This village seemed a
twin to Bir Zebbuggia where my family
vacationed in the summer when I was a child.
As it was right 'next door', we soon arrived at
Bir Zebbuggia and I tried very hard to locate
our summer home. I was not successful
although I did recognize the area where small
flats were still being used by tourists.
Although only a few miles from Tarxien,
where we lived, we moved to Bir Zebbuggia
every summer. We had a small flat across the
bay and enjoyed a very different lifestyle from
that of Tarxien. Of course, school was out and
my dad, who worked closer here than from
our winter home, took advantage of the area

by taking us on many boat rides. He had his own boat and, as he was quite good with motors, was continuously improving it. The boat was fairly large and, I'm sure at my mom's bidding, he used it to take large groups of nuns and orphans who resided in a nearby orphanage for nice long boat rides. In turn, my sister Mary and I were constantly gifted with lovely crocheted dresses made by the nuns. Other boat excursions included my dad taking us out and diving for sea urchins, which we then enjoyed fresh and raw on the boat. I examined a sea urchin recently and couldn't imagine my eating it, raw, at that time. Another hobby of my dad's, during the summer, was to collect sea salt. He would anchor the boat on a rocky deserted area that had many holes in the rocks.

He would then pour sea water into the holes and let the sun evaporate the seawater and create sea salt. I don't know the exact time lapse for this process but he did collect salt often because once the water evaporated, the result was immediately salt. Little did he know that many years later sea salt would become the 'in' salt used by this country.

Another memory I connect with Bir Zebbuggia is the death of my baby brother Louis Victor. My mother had already lost two baby boys, at birth, before I was born so after two girls, my dad was overjoyed to have another boy. As it turned out, while we were vacationing by the sea, my little 8-month-old brother took sick. After a lot of medication, and a lot of worrying, he died and as was the custom, he was laid out in our living room for a day until burial. It was so sad, to see Louis Victor in a little white coffin. Mom and Dad sat with him all night, unable to hide their grief, unable to sleep. They just watched their son until it was time to bury him the next day.

Imagine the horror when Dad went to the photo store to pick up weekly photos and discovered ones of Louis Victor, a laughing baby, and he was already buried!

***

My dad often reminded us that, in certain areas of Malta, he had to take the boat farther out because, as he told us, Malta was once the top of a land bridge from Sicily to Africa and driving a boat close to this area would cause us to hit the sunken bridge extending to Sicily.

***

Bir Zebbugia has now become a very active area with lots of cranes and other implements for marine commerce. It had always been very industrial, in fact, during the war when Dad worked here, he worked on torpedoes. Now, in the modern world, it was even more so. Here we stopped at a farmer's market where, in addition to fruit and vegetables there were lovely linens and embroidery on display, definitely for the tourists. I guess many Maltese ladies spent their free time embroidering tablecloths and such because every village seemed to have its own display of these Maltese crafts for the tourists.

***

We had a seaside lunch among the fishing boats. As I'm sure you've noticed, because Malta is a small island, just about every restaurant is located near the water and serves, as its main entrees, fish. While I enjoyed lunch, all these memories of the past came back to me.

After lunch, our usual plan was to stay a while with a glass of wine, the pungent salty air further relaxing us, before we started traveling again. Today turned out to be a very busy day. It was hot and the heat tired us quickly but we trudged on. Our goal to see most of Malta in two weeks was not to be taken lightly although we did take a lot of drink breaks in between the places we visited.

Now, in the afternoon, we were ready to go to the eastern coast area. But first, we headed inland to Tarxien where I lived as a child. I had a dual purpose in visiting Tarxien. Besides it being the village where I spent my childhood, it also housed an important megalithic temple, a prehistoric site dating from c.4,000 to 2,500 BC. This temple was not a tourist attraction when I lived in Tarxien as a child. In fact, my friends and I used to play among the rocks, which, now, are protected and untouchable. As a matter of fact, I remembered exactly where it was in relations to my house. I used to walk there as a child.

We would get together after school, walk to the rocks and play *house* or hide and seek and other children's games. When I think of all the times, we squeezed and sneaked around the now important and untouchable altars and other structures of the temples I have to laugh at the very uncaring way we played on these now holy and precious prehistoric stones.

In addition, on the border of Tarxien, in Paola, is the Hypogeum, an underground burial site dating from the same time as the temple and recognized as a World Heritage Site. We had to time our visit here as this specific site requires advance online booking by date and time. Only eight persons are permitted to enter at a time.

It was hard going down the roughly carved steps, two flights down in semi darkness, to arrive at the large chamber that was probably used for funerary gatherings. The site covers three stories below ground, all hewn from rock by crude tools. It is literally an underground cemetery. Our small group was led down these rough, narrow steps, slowly, until we reached the bottom level. In one of the larger chambers, the guide told us that visitors can call out and hear their voices echo around the great room. Naturally, we all did. It sounded very eerie. It reminded me of when the Wizard spoke to the four visitors in Oz.

Whatever caused this phenomenon, it must have worked well for the high priests who oversaw the place at that time. It caused an otherworldly sound, especially, I imagine, to primitive people. Did I mention? It works better on male voices.

This ancient Hypogeum is definitely well worth the visit but it must be booked quite a bit in advance and there is literally no parking lot nearby. One has to do with street parking which is not exactly great in these small villages.

After visiting these two ancient sites, it was time to visit a site from the very recent past, about 65 years ago, my home. I knocked on the door of 21 St. Anthony Street and a nice-looking lady opened the door. Her name was Rosanna. As I had been there five years earlier, she remembered me. "How are you?"

she said and I again identified myself and she greeted me warmly. Seems that she was the last of her family; I had met her mom the last time but she had passed a few years ago.

Rosanna's mother had purchased this house from my mother before we sailed to New York over fifty years ago! She welcomed me and my friend and cousins who were showing us around Malta. She gave us a tour of my past home, showing it to my cousins who were not even born when I left Malta. I added to the tour by explaining how we had used each room and how we had lived in the house. Rosanna told me that her mother had added another room, expanded the kitchen, and enclosed the bathroom into the house. She also changed the stairway to the roof.

When I lived there, we had to go out into the yard to use the bathroom and it had a pull chain from the top to flush.

It's amazing to think that my mom had sold this house to Rosanna's mom and she had lived there all that time. I was even more surprised when I saw, in the living room, the same beautiful blue-and-white tile that my grandmother had placed there. It was still beautiful, the colors still vibrant after at least seventy-five years. "Everybody who sees that tile remarks on how beautiful and bright it still is after all this time," she said. That was true; I myself found it hard to believe that it was the same tile but I had photos of my Communion party, in 1948, 67 years ago, and I can see that it was the same. I should add, as an aside, that the beverage of choice at my communion party was wine. We did not drink soda and wine was the drink that accompanied all our meals. As in most of Europe, children were brought up drinking a small portion of wine. There was no rush to 'get drunk' when one reached a certain age as in countries where one did not taste wine as a child.

We only used this room for rare occasions. The last time we used it was for laying out my nana when she died before we came to the United States. There were no funeral parlors in Malta at that time and when a person died, they were laid out in the living room of their home and friends and neighbors paid their respects there.

***

I went up to the roof where I had played as a
child. Those steep stairs were still a bit
treacherous even though Rosanna's mother
had altered the stairway. I recalled all the
times I had run up the stairs and squeezed
into the rabbit hutch which was built midway
up the stairs. I would go there when my dad
was upset with me and ready to do a bit of
punishment. However, as he couldn't get into
the hutch as I had, I was saved from whatever
punishment he had intended. Unfortunately,
the hutch had been removed but I still
remembered cuddling with the cute bunnies
not realizing that they were being raised to be
dinner someday.

Up on the roof, I'd had photos taken with my sister and my grandmother when I was nine and brought them with me. I posed in the exact same place and now I have two photos on my old roof, one taken in 1949 and the other in 2015. Other than the change in my age, the roof and balconies across from our house remain the same. Stonework, which is the basis for all construction in Malta, seems to survive for ages. I'm sure that this house, solid as it has been all this time, was but a baby compared to the structures that we had explored in Valletta earlier.

From this rooftop, I remembered that I used to play with my girlfriend, Yvonne, who lived across the street. We communicated, she from her second story balcony, I, on my roof.

We'd call to each other and were able to carry on a conversation in those old days of no phones. Obviously, we did not have the Internet then either. Another memory also triggered by my being on the roof was that of my much younger days, during the war. My dad used to take me up to the roof so that we can see the bombs coming down all over the island. To my child's mind, I considered the bombs as fireworks; they were all lit up as they came down. At that time, I never connected the beautiful display in the sky with the terrible devastation that followed on the ground.

Once we came down from the roof, Rosanna gave us some refreshments as we chatted about 'our' house. I also asked

Rosanna about my godmother, Giovanna, who lived next door. The house was under construction now; nobody lived there but Rosanna told me about what went on there as well as mentioning other neighbors that I had remembered. It was a nostalgic session.

***

This house awakened in me all sorts of memories. Many an afternoon I would sit on our stoop with my grandmother as she taught me to crochet and knit. She also taught me how to make Maltese lace, lace that is still being sold in Malta as a unique creation of the Maltese people. Making this lace required having a long straw-filled object much like a long skinny pillow, many skinny spools to hold the silk thread and, of course, a pattern. I still remember how proud I was when I learned this very Maltese tradition. I even had Maltese lace collars on some of my dresses as the original purpose for this lace was to embellish the aristocracy's clothing and it is still doing that job today. It is a beautiful and intricate art form that is recognized throughout as a specialty of Malta.

Other memories of my house include the fact that in our last year living here, it was just my mom, my nana and my sister and I. Where was my dad? That story started a while ago, just after World War II ended.

***

My father was concerned about the future of his two daughters. Malta was a bit unsettled at the time. We were rewarded the *George Cross* for valiant fighting and bravery but it still didn't improve the country for the Maltese people. First, there was the after-the-war devastation. Buildings were bombed and had not yet been rebuilt. And, most important, there was no way a citizen could move up in the world. So, my dad, started planning on taking his family to the United States, where the streets were lined in gold and great opportunities existed for immigrants.

In those days, one needed a sponsor just to come to the States. Dad knew a Maltese family friend, Leli, who had a relative living in New York. He said he would ask him to sponsor my dad and give him a job. So, the next time Justin visited his family in Malta, Dad made his acquaintance and convinced him to be his sponsor.

I still remember meeting Justin's family, his two daughters, Irene and Rita, when we attended a party given by Justin in his beautiful and never seen before giant yacht. I remember this distinctly because I had to attend the party in a black dress, another story.

My mom, who was constantly making deals with God, promised that I, who had been quite sick for some time, would wear a black dress every Wednesday for a year if I was healed. And, I was, so, I ended up wearing the plain black dress on that Wednesday, at this very special party where everyone was dressed in fancy clothes. Needless to say, I was a bit embarrassed but mom wouldn't let me wear anything else.

After submitting applications, filling in forms and having Justin's guarantee of a position in one of his hotels in New York City, Dad was finally placed on a list of future immigrants to the United States.

He couldn't leave immediately as there was some sort of law that only a certain number of emigrants can enter the United States from each country in Europe annually and Dad had to wait his turn.

Finally, that day came and Dad traveled to the United States to set up a home for us. The position he had been promised to be allowed in the country, even though he was an engineer, ended up his shoveling coal in a NYC hotel. Anything to come to this country. What a difference today!

While in the States, for a year before we arrived, Dad would send us clothing from America. How proud we were to be dressed in American clothes! I still remember the very colorful socks that he sent us once. We never took them off!

***

Standing outside my former home, which was on a corner of St. Anthony Street, I could look across the street to the other corner. Here, on the ground, was a large patch of concrete. It was here that we trudged, on a daily basis, into an underground shelter, during the war. It was also here that my younger sister, Mary, was born, in the shelter, during a bombing and it was also from this corner that we started our trek to the parish church in Tarxien to have Mary baptized.

"How much farther," I would ask as we walked and walked to get to the parish church. No cars and definitely no gas was available at the time so we had to walk. I don't know the distance but, to me, very young at the time, it took forever. And, while in this shelter area, I still had a vivid memory of an injury I sustained. Today, I still see the results on my hand. I was very young at the time, a toddler, and I was crawling on the shelter floor one night, during a bombing. My dad, ever prepared as men had to be at that time, by wearing some heavy boots, accidently stepped on my hands and, as I pulled my hand back, one of my nails remained under the boot. The tip of my finger is still bent because of this injury. A forever reminder of that time, during the war.

It was in the other direction, down St. Anthony Street, that I walked daily to my convent school. The street looked so narrow now, seeing it with adult eyes. I took piano lessons at school, and played and made friends. I can still recall the practice sessions that I had to endure on the piano, instead of recess, during my lunchtime. Since we could not afford a piano and piano lessons require practice, I had to do this daily. Again, it was down this same street that I chased my grandmother's funeral carriage because I wanted to attend her burial and was told that I was too young. In those days, the funeral carriage was glass enclosed, showing the casket within, with horses pulling it so that it made quite an impressive cortege.

Another event, which happened not long after nana's funeral, was my birthday celebration, the last birthday in Malta. Since my nana had passed, we were now ready to come join Dad in the United States. Nana had refused to leave the country of her birth so we had to wait with her. As a surprise, Dad ordered a birthday cake for me, from a bakery. Wow! I never had had a bakery cake before. It was decorated beautifully and just about everyone on our block stopped by to see it. I had a wonderful birthday party although a bit subdued because we had buried nana not long before. That was one of my last memories of my home in Malta. We all had mixed feelings at that time; sad because we lost our nana, happy because we were going to join Dad in the states. Really, visiting here was quite an assault on my memories. I exchanged names and emails with Rosanna and we promised each other to stay in touch.

Now it was around suppertime and Joe suggested that we have dinner at a new place called Smart City Malta. Rarely seen in Malta, or in all of Europe, this new city was a complete new creation of this decade. It was not built on remains of another place, it was a fresh start and a really new place.

It was quite interesting, with many new buildings and a fantastic color fountain with great music. The dancing waters were the best that I had ever seen, even better than the ones in Las Vegas.

The waters danced to classical style music and the colors changed continuously so that the whole performance was a feast for both the ears and the eyes. Later, we ate at The Londoner, which, of course, had British fare.

We all had fish and chips and wine and lingered till dark. We spent quite a few hours enjoying this spectacle until it got late, we got tired and we were very happy to say good bye to a lovely day!

We got back to our hotel fairly late in the evening. Europeans tend to eat much later than we do in the States. We had time for a nightcap, again at the Penthouse Lounge, and then retired for the day. It was a long and beautiful day. Besides my memories from long ago, I was creating new and exciting memories of Malta.

Day 6 – Thursday, Harbor Cruise

I have not mentioned our breakfasts in Sliema. We enjoyed a quiet, light breakfast and, as such, we found a couple of nice grocery stores where we were able to purchase our needs and enjoy a leisurely breakfast in our room. Of course, we always included the ever-famous Maltese bread. To me, it was a relaxing way to start the day.

Today we decided to begin by going on a Valletta/Three Cities Harbor Cruise. It was refreshing to be on a boat, in the shade and on the water on another hot day, which it turned out to be.

***

We toured the Grand Harbor, one of the best harbors in all of Europe. The harbor comprises of Valletta, the Capital, as well as Senglea, Vittoriosa and Birgu, the original Three Cities. This time, we took the bus to Valletta. When we were ready to return, we took the bus back to Sliema. Malta's transportation system, which is basically made up of busses, is very easy to use. All busses start and end in Valletta in a giant terminal just out of the Capital City's main gate. Of course, there are always taxis, and, for the tourists, carozzin, horse drawn carriages for short, leisurely travel. If you need to go a distance, there are also car rentals but beware, Malta is still governed by British driving rules; that is, cars drive in the opposite direction from all other European countries and this may take a bit of time to adjust to. We had a couple of near accidents ourselves when we rented a car.

On the harbor cruise, we enjoyed the refreshing sea breeze which was more than welcome on the hot day that it had become. We traveled along the many branches of the harbor, which seemed like fingers stretching out over the land. We sailed around the two natural harbors as well as the ten creeks located on either side of Valletta. We traveled through a dry dock area, where various ships and oil rigs were being repaired. We passed several marinas with million-dollar yachts; they were very lovely to look at and we wondered who owned these fantastic vessels. We went past a few giant cruise ships dropping off their guests for a day in Malta. As we were touring Valletta from the water, we saw many of the forts that were useful, ages ago, when the Maltese people and the Knights of Malta were struggling to prevent enemies from taking over their country. Fort St. Elmo, at the tip of Valletta is the most prominent. We had already stopped here earlier and would eventually come back later.

Schooners and smaller pleasure boats finish the variety of watercraft we enjoyed seeing on this cruise. When I see the architecture of European cities, the forts, castles and great walls, I find it humbling that in my new country, the oldest buildings weren't even considered when these structures were built. As in much of Europe, buildings in Malta are generally from the Middle Ages, the Renaissance or before, and it is amazing to see that most of them are still in excellent shape.

***

As I enjoyed the harbor cruise, I found it hard to imagine that when I was a child here, during the War, ships would arrive from England loaded with food for the starving

Maltese people. My parents, with most of the Maltese, would watch in horror as each ship was bombed by the enemy and the food which we so badly needed sank into the harbor.

We were very hungry at this time because the foods, which were generally imported from neighboring countries, never got to Malta during the war. My grandmother, in particular, nearly starved to death because she would not eat food from the Victory Kitchens, food that was prepared by strangers, unknown to her. She was very picky and got to be very skinny!

Because the harbor cruise was such a pleasant experience, we decided to book the cruise around Malta. We were told by several of the guests on this cruise that the Malta cruise was well worth taking so we managed to book it for the next day and were looking forward to being on the water again.

***

After the harbor cruise, we went back to our hotel for a late lunch at the hotel pool Tiki Hut and enjoyed a very comfortable stay by the water. The pool and snack bar were across the main street from our hotel and were situated next to the Mediterranean Sea. The pool water comes from the sea itself and is very salty and coolly refreshing. As a rule, the beaches in Malta are very rocky and steep. There are a few sandy beaches but here in Sliema, our pool and the accompanying beach on which it was built tended to be rocky. The facilities were very comfortable with the Tiki Hut serving many of our favorites for our lunch choices. We were content with our hamburgers, French fries, and a nice cold drink and treated ourselves to a very relaxing and laid-back afternoon. We were getting used to relaxing, but had quite a few more days left in Malta and still plenty to see. After lunch and a swim, we were energized enough to go to our hotel room, change and get ready to be picked up by my cousins who invited us to their home for a barbeque.

***

This barbeque was different from any American barbeques we were used to. My relatives lived in Mosta. So, Joe picked us up and drove us to his house. Houses, in Malta, are built of stone and usually look like row houses. There are not many single, separate houses. They maintain their privacy with high walls around their backyards. They decorate their backyards beautifully with trees, planters, and structures to make spending the time there very comfortable. The high walls also serve another purpose as, except for noontime, there is shade, very welcome shade in the hot summer sun.

Our feast started with smoked fish appetizers, salmon, tuna, squid, and other delicacies. As it was late in the day, we had no problem with the hot sun. The plantings around the area lent an ambiance of pleasant relaxation and the welcoming family members made us feel totally comfortable. Being entertained in my cousins' backyard was a very different experience from home in our backyards and lanais. A fountain on the back wall added the soothing sounds as we sat enjoying our first drinks of the occasion. The high walls around the yard worked well to ensure our privacy. Very European!

Justin, the son, brought previously marinated tuna steaks and cooked them to perfection. Maria, the daughter, who was attending law school at the time, created an interestingly yummy dip by using two cheeses and beer and they served galletti, a hard, crisp cracker which I hadn't seen since I was a child, with the other nibbles, chips, nuts and stuff.

With the tuna, they served a green and red pepper dish, an eggplant dish as well as a pasta salad. This dinner was very filling and, with the wine served, we could hardly move. After dinner, we enjoyed conversation into the night and we were getting tired. Again, as in Europe, these dinners are served very late, way too late for our usual dining habit.

But, we had not seen the end of dinner yet. The cheese course accompanied by fruit followed and after that, ice cream. We enjoyed ourselves tremendously. We had a lovely dinner with lovely company. I certainly should be proud of my Maltese relatives. They are extremely well educated and terrific people besides. We couldn't have had a better time and, after midnight, were more than ready to go to our hotel and enjoy a good night's sleep.

We felt fortunate that for this event, we were picked up and driven back home by family. It allowed us to relax more, and enjoy more wine, than we would have if we were getting back to the hotel on our own.

In two days, we head for Mellieha and the other hotel, a timeshare. We again had a full day with many new memories as well as old ones, renewed.

Day 7 – Friday, Cruise to Gozo and Comino

Today we woke up looking forward to a full day on the water, the cruise to Gozo and Comino. The recommended cruise was run by Captain Morgan Cruises and consisted of a ride on a beautiful Turkish gullet, The Fernandes.

We were picked up at our hotel, for a small fee, and taken to the gullet. It was a beautiful schooner with a very large forward deck, a covered stern deck and a fairly large saloon. This was a day cruise and everyone on board was excited and ready to enjoy a full day at sea. Soon, we left the Sliema Marina and cruised northward toward Gozo. We were on our way.

It is very different to see the places we visited from the water. After leaving Sliema, we rounded the coast and could see the sea view of the Hilton and the Radisson hotels. We had once stayed in both and again, it was a completely different view. It was smooth sailing and we passed various harbors including St. Julian's, St. Paul's Bay and

Mellieha Bay. In between these bays, we encountered a few panoramic cliffs, inlets and coves. One of the first attractions we passed, and one that we did not intend to visit, was Popeye's Village, just before Mellieha. This attraction had grown from a film set for the 1980 musical production into one of the major tourist attractions in Malta. It has been converted into a Fun Park and consists of a collection of ramshackle huts and wooden shacks that were originally Popeye's home.

It is actually the only film set still standing, in all of Europe, and it has become a must on tourists' *to do* lists.

Just before noontime, we dropped anchor on a secluded bay in Gozo. Once anchored, some of us spent time swimming and snorkeling, others, sunbathing and relaxing on the spacious decks.

At lunch, we were treated to a sumptuous buffet on the schooner. It was pretty lavish for lunch on a boat. We had grilled steak, fish and a large selection of hot vegetables. In addition, there were selections of cold meats and salads as well as fresh fruit, wine, soda and unlimited beer. No complaints here!

After that sumptuous meal, everyone was ready to relax. We sailed to Comino. The third island of the Maltese archipelago, again dropping anchor at the Blue Lagoon. We spent the whole afternoon here, swimming in the crystal waters of the lagoon. I might add here that in Malta, as well as other Mediterranean islands, there seem to be many

Blue Lagoons. It must be that the Mediterranean Sea, in many locations, breeds this kind of clear, beautiful phosphorescent waters that are titled as such.

***

For the daring, there was an optional Jet Boat trip to take us closer, in and around the caves of Comino. Not realizing, what was involved, we booked this optional trip. It was a scary trip! The captain, to make it more exciting, or probably to scare the women on board, sped the small boat and leaned it on its side.

The women, myself included, screamed as we thought that the boat was going to flip. I, a non-swimmer was already searching for the life preservers. The captain, and some of the

97

men, thought it was funny. After that thrilling ride, it was pleasant to enjoy the slow cruise into the caves where the phosphorescent waters were even more brilliant. They seemed magical! Still anchored at Comino, we enjoyed the afternoon, snacking on fresh fruit, sunbathing and taking advantage of a fully stocked bar. What a life!

In a while, we started sailing again. More cold drinks made the return trip as comfortable and pleasant as anyone could expect on this fantastic schooner. Soon, we docked and were on land again. We were transported back to the hotel and planned on a fairly quiet evening. The hot sun had tired us out.

We were actually too full to dine out this evening, so we simply walked a bit around the promenade, had some ice cream and people watched for a while. Not far from our hotel was a small salon where people were paying to have fish nibble on their feet. It was supposed to be soothing. We stopped to watch for a while. They sat in these comfortable chairs, like shoe shine parlors and dipped their feet into transparent plastic tubs with fish in them. It seemed a bit weird but they were enjoying the feeling. It must have been ticklish at times.

Once at our hotel we settled at the bar with a nice gin and tonic and listened to relaxing music all evening.

Day 8 – Saturday, Mellieha

Today we changed our view. We left the Preluna Hotel and proceeded, with Joe and Liz's help to go to Mellieha and set up living at the Pergola Resort and Spa. The amenities offered and the apartment itself pleasantly surprised us. Since this was a timeshare, we had a large area with a living room, bedroom and kitchen included. It was quite nice!

Mellieha was also a surprise in that it was very hilly. I had been to Malta many times but never in this area so it was very new to me. My only remembrance of Mellieha was when I was very young, after the war. Mom, who was notorious at making deals with God and his mother, had made a promise when my dad was nearly paralyzed. She promised that if he would be able to walk again, she would take him on a pilgrimage to a special church dedicated to the Blessed Mother in Mellieha. He did get better and, true to her word, she and Dad went on an 18-mile pilgrimage from Bir Zebbuggia to Mellieha. She was very religious and very persuasive to convince my dad to make such a journey.

***

Just an example of how hilly Mellieha was, the Preluna Hotel and Spa occupied seven stories and all of them went out to the street. The street itself is made up of stairs and spans the seven stories. It seems hard to imagine! We entered through the lobby which turned out to be the seventh floor. The first floor was downhill and also had a street entrance. A little weird at first but we quickly got used to it. We dropped off our luggage and explored the hotel. It had three pools, on different floors and I swam a bit while Bob relaxed in the room. After we had a good swim, Joe and Liz came back to take us around St. Paul's Bay, where St. Paul was originally shipwrecked on his way to Rome and martyrdom. A wild storm had directed his ship to a safe harbor in Malta and he proceeded to Christianize the pagans living there. We walked around the bay area, a much quieter place than Sliema. Some tourists prefer this area for that reason. While Sliema is active and very populated, Mellieha is quiet and relaxing. We had a lovely lunch at an outdoor café called Watercolours. Liz and I had salmon baguettes while the guys had octopus salads which Bob enjoyed very much. We were also able to enjoy some FaceTime with our families in the States.

Before we returned to the hotel, Joe and Liz gave us a tour of their vacation condo. It seemed strange to us, in the States, for anyone living on such a small island to have two homes, one being a vacation home. They had to be no more than 5 or 6 miles away from each other. But then, when I lived in Malta we had the same situation. We lived in Tarxien, a small village inland but, in the summers, we moved to Bir Zebbuggia, on the water, a smaller place but much cooler with the sea breezes.

***

Later, we went back to the hotel and spent the full afternoon with more swimming and walking around town, exploring. Since this was a Timeshare, and we had a kitchen, we tried to warm up some scones for a snack and heat some water for tea. We were not very successful and had to call a maintenance man to show us how to work the appliances. They were very different from what we were used to in the States. Later, we were invited to a cocktail party for the time share members. It was pleasant meeting future friends from all over the world. We enjoyed meeting Carol and Phil from England and we chatted with them for a while. They seemed to be well traveled and were planning to go to Kenya next year.

Later in the evening we had plans to have a nice dinner with Joe and Liz. Joe had been very good to us; he took us all over and what we usually did with the Hop On Hop Off busses, we did again with Joe, in an obviously more convenient and detailed setting with family. We also received personal information and facts, more than one would receive on the Hop On Hop Off busses. And, of course, seeing all the attractions more than once, embedded them deeper in our memories.

We went to dinner at Paulus, an outdoor restaurant in St. Paul's Bay, which specialized in fish. I had mussels as an appetizer, the others had calamari and then we all ordered sea bass, cooked with a salt coating. When it was done, they presented the whole, large, cooked fish to us and later, proceeded to fillet it for our dining pleasure. We were presented with a delicious white fish serving. It really tasted fresh. We enjoyed it with quite a bit of wine. All in all, another perfect ending to another perfect day. Weather-wise, we had been very lucky. Every day was more glorious than the previous one. The evening breezes had enhanced our dining experience as we had dined on an outside patio.

The only glitch to the evening happened when we were parking. Joe hit the curb with one of the tires and we heard an ominous hiss. We were afraid he had gotten a flat but upon examination it turned out that he had hit the valve and had let out some air.

He checked the tire on several occasions that evening, but it did not release any more air. It never went down, so we were hoping that he wouldn't have to replace it.

Soon after, Joe drove us to our new home, tired but happy to be enjoying Malta so much!

While in our room, we received a phone call from my cousin Richard. He invited us to dinner, tomorrow at the restaurant in Mdina. Something to look forward to, for sure!

That event concluded our adventure for the night.

Day 9 – Sunday, St. Julian's Feast

This morning brought its own new issues. It being Sunday, we made plans to go to the Festa at St. Julian's and attend Mass in a nearby chapel. In Malta, it seems that every weekend, some village celebrates a Festa. This feast celebrates St. Julian, the patron saint of the parish church and Malta has a lot of churches and as a result, a lot of Festas.

***

St. Julian's is the village adjoining Sliema so we planned to return to familiar grounds, by bus, for our enjoyment of this celebration. We had a leisurely breakfast, (pastizzi for me!) and got ready to pick up the bus for St. Julian's. This village, like most of the villages on the eastern shores of Malta, has a small, very scenic bay with traditional fishing boats, the dajhsas, and is lined around the water with numerous bars, restaurants and hotels. This area contains the most five-star hotels on the island. And, as with Sliema, St. Julian's has its own tree lined promenade encouraging tourists and natives alike to stroll and enjoy the sun dappled coastline.

Surprise! There was no bus transportation to St. Julian's because the streets in the village celebrating a Festa are closed to transportation. This is done so that so that the people can stroll around town comfortably. Also, the parade, with gorgeously costumed resident bands and many statues representing the patron saints will be marching throughout the streets of the village. Once we realized that our bus was not taking us all the way to St. Julian's, we had to alter our plans; the bus would stop at the nearest area, which was close to Paceville and then we would have to walk from there.

This detour actually worked for us because the chapel in which we planned to attend mass was close by. We had been there last Sunday, so it was easy to find. We were lucky to have timed it correctly, just by sheer luck.

Later, we had to decide how to get to St. Julian's and the festa.

I, a walker by habit, was willing to walk but my friend was not in favor of this, as it seemed a very long trip going around the many mini harbors to get from one town to the other. However, there was another option. We were given a local map and discovered that if we went in a straight line, not hugging the serpentine coastline but traveling through the village itself, we were able to get to St. Julian's in half the time and luckily, I was able to convince Bob to walk this shorter version, which we did.

It really wasn't a long walk, but, as I've already mentioned, the whole world was very hot that summer, Malta included. Since we walked in a sunny area, we ended up hot and tired before we got to the parade and Festa area in St. Julian's.

I was quite familiar with this area as I had stayed here on two of my previous trips to Malta. This is the area where the Hilton Hotel is located – a beautiful and resort-like place where I had stayed with my daughter on my last trip.

Once here, we took a break for a light snack and a nice cold drink while we watched and listened to the exotically costumed and very colorful bands march and play their beautiful music. We also enjoyed people

115

watching and hearing the variety of languages that were being spoken by the many European tourists in town. Later, once the festivities were partially over, (they go on all night!) we asked some locals about the possibility of a bus going in our needed direction and were told that up the hill and a bit to the left there was a bus waiting for passengers to board and would be leaving soon. It was actually not far from where we had gotten off originally. The bus was going to Paceville, a pleasure center of Malta where there are many hotels, restaurants, cafes, bars, discos, and cinemas. It is a hopping place, mostly for the younger tourists, a lively part of Malta year-round.

I had been to Paceville before and weren't sure whether we'd have time to go there on this trip. There was loud music, lots of fast food places and crowds all over.

We got to our hotel in due time and had a late lunch of antipasti by our hotel pool. After such a long trip to St. Julian's we decided to take it easy and enjoyed another swimming afternoon in the pool. We relaxed; something we really needed to do more of while in Malta. It was good that our dinner with Richard and Emily was going to be late. We needed time to get organized for going out to dinner with family again. We picked up on the general idea that dinner with family involved a lot of eating. We realized that we were eating way too much on this vacation, so

117

a dinner fast was appropriate; however, it was not going to happen today!

***

Later that evening, Richard and his wife, Emily, picked us up at our hotel and took us to dine at Bacchus, a lovely open-air restaurant in the old city of Mdina. Seeing Mdina at night was so different from being there during the day. There are no tourists around and we could really see why the name, The Silent City, was so appropriate. It was extremely quiet with almost no one around. We walked through the two gigantic doors at the main gate. Once in a while, we'd hear the echoing footsteps of fellow restaurant goers as they trod through the maze of narrow streets that is Mdina. Being here, one gets the distinct feeling of being transported into the fourteenth century, into a medieval town. This is the city that could not be penetrated by the Turks in *The Great Siege*. And, in this place, was the most fantastic restaurant. The Bacchus is an upscale restaurant, laid out in the original structures with barrel vaults and heavy stone walls. We dined in the gardens, actually on the roof, with canopies over the tables. Richard's adult children, Veronica and Jean Pierre were also there. The service was impeccable. We had a lovely, late dinner here, enjoyed steak and stuffed rabbit. The portions were perfect and the service was excellent. It was a great dining experience as we spent the evening catching up with these relatives, this time from my mom's side of the family. It's nice to get together with family, especially family members that we had not seen for quite a while. Again, we were totally tired when we said goodnight and were driven to our hotel by Richard and Emily.

Day 10 – Monday, Mellieha Bay

Today was what we determined to be a free day. No traveling around the country, we just decided to have a leisurely day 'at the beach.'

We chose to go to Mellieha Bay because it is one of the few beaches in Malta that is made up of sand and now it was much closer than before. It seems strange to discuss the closeness of a place when the whole island is so small but, when in Malta, distance seems to be different. And, for whatever reason, maybe because the roads meander, traveling takes so much longer than on our easy to use highways. Malta, overall, is made up of rocky beaches and Mellieha is that much more attractive because it is unique in that it is sandy. Going to Mellieha from our new home was an easy trip, and fairly short. We waited for the bus right by our hotel and enjoyed the ride, listening to the natives speak Maltese and knowing that they did not realize I could understand whatever they were saying. It was fun.

We rented some chairs and umbrellas, brought a light picnic lunch, a few books and thoroughly enjoyed the day. Off and on we could hear various languages. Malta is the beach location of choice for many Europeans.

We heard languages from Holland, Germany, England, and Italy enjoying the Maltese weather. We just got very lazy and spent the whole day at the beach. Somewhat sunburned, we returned to our hotel in time for dinner. We did not want to travel too much today so we stayed close to our hotel. It was relaxing to change and shower and not be too tired to move as we have been lately from all our roaming. And, we did plan to eat a bit less. The restaurant we chose was called Tosca. We found it as we were strolling through Mellieha.

It was previously recommended by another hotel. This time, we enjoyed fresh fish, again, as the restaurant had them as a specialty. In fact, as we entered the restaurant, the head waiter brought us some fish that had been caught that morning so, naturally, we chose fish. The prices were very good for the excellent service we received and the staff was friendly and courteous. Being in the water and sun all day made us tired and it was good to walk back to our hotel, easily and quickly, and make it an early bedtime for a change. Tomorrow we plan to do lunch at my cousin Lydia's.

Day 11 – Tuesday, Balzan, San Anton Gardens

As it turned out, today was another day that we were on our own. Joe has been unable to drive us for a few days so we decided to rent a car and be truly 'on our own' for a day or so. But first, I wanted to start the day right. I went to the gym to exercise. I had been eating a lot! Our timeshare had a very well-equipped gym and I felt great and very invigorated having gone through a bit of a workout, similar to what I usually do at home. Now I won't feel so guilty at lunch and dinner.

Traveling from Mellieha by bus would have been fine but, we decided, to do a bit more exploring and see what it's like to drive on the 'wrong' side of the street, as in England. Driving in this manner is a leftover from the days when Malta was a British Protectorate and, I suppose, it will never change. It was an adventure to learn to drive like this. We were constantly looking in the wrong direction when making a turn and then, to make things even worse, we were confronted with a multitude of roundabouts, all going, for us, the wrong way.

One thing about Maltese roads, they are not numbered as our roads here are. When we got to a roundabout, we saw the name of the next town at each exit. As we were not familiar with all the towns involved, we ended up going round and round on the roundabouts. For an island that is 19 miles at its longest, it took us over two hours to reach my cousin's house from our hotel, a distance of mere miles.

We had been invited for lunch and, as we finally reached our destination, in the village of Balzan, we were at my cousin Lydia's house. I remembered the house from when I was a little girl, and we visited our aunt Censina a long time ago. People don't move very often in Malta. Being in the same house where I had visited as a child brought more memories to me. It obviously was an older home and, since it was attached on both sides, it did not have much light until we went out to the yard. Here were a multitude of plants, flowers and small trees. The Maltese take advantage of every small space to grow all sorts of flowers. It looked beautiful and very colorful.

My cousin barely recognized me as, this time, I was a blonde. Lydia and I are close in age and, when I was in Malta as a child, we played together at all the family functions. It seemed weird to meet again as older ladies. We had a nice lunch, which included a delicious meat pie accompanied by fresh vegetables and fruit for dessert. It was a nice change from all the seafood we had been eating.

After lunch, Lydia joined us as we went for a drive in her village and then planned to tour San Anton Gardens. The roads here are really narrow. As an example, as we were driving on one street, we could extend our arms and touch both side walls. I grazed my hands reaching out to touch the walls. I guess these roads definitely do not allow two-way traffic and if a car is on the road, another car coming in the opposite direction must wait, at the corner until it passes. I saw similar situations in rural England.

Narrow, cobblestone roads and stonewalls seem to be the way the roads were built in small villages in Malta.

Later, we went to San Anton Gardens, a nearby, historic garden that we visited during the Hop On Hop Off tour. We again enjoyed leisurely strolls among the beautiful exotic trees and flowers. The garden had a very nice exhibit of interesting plants and has been open to the public since 1882.

We spent the day walking around this beautiful setting until it was time to drive back to our hotel and relax. After a day of driving, unlike any we had done before, it was good to get back 'home'. I must include that the new experience of driving in Malta brought with it the horrendous experience of trying to park in Malta. Especially in Sliema, parking was just a bit above hopeless. It took us quite a bit of time to find a place to park and once parked, we walked rather than move the car from place to place. We were soon getting the hang of driving the British way and headed for our hotel in Mellieha easily. In two days, we will return our rented car in Valletta, enjoy a day in the capital city, and then, get together with my cousins for an evening dinner.

***

Tonight, we dined in a local restaurant, very near our original hotel in Sliema. We missed the hustle and bustle and crowds of Sliema and since Balzan was not so far from Sliema, we thought to go back there one more time. The restaurant was one that was originally recommended by our hotel staff. Ta' Kris is a small restaurant and not too easy to find as it was in an alley near the Sliema Ferries. It served traditional Maltese food with generous portions. The staff was very friendly and seemed happy to be working there. The menu had quite a bit of variety for a small restaurant and the fish we ordered (lampuki) were very good. It was nice to take another stroll after dinner along the Sliema waterfront and stop for gelati. Mellieha is much quieter and there are no crowds strolling the shoreline. Every day we seem to have a full day with many new memories as well as old ones, renewed.

Day 12 – Wednesday, The Northwest Malta

This morning, while we were still on our own, with a car, we decided to rough it by exploring the northwest area of Malta. Looking at a map, one sees there are no roads that hug the coast. If one wants to explore this not too populated side of Malta, one must meander back and forth through the very rocky spots and pass through some of the small villages.

From Mellieha, and with a map in hand, it was easy to see our route. We headed northwest and aimed for Paradise Bay. This bay is the northernmost part of the island. It is near here where one takes the ferry for Gozo.

We were saving that trip for another day so we just stopped and enjoyed the view. It would have been nice to drive along the coast but there are no easy roads here so we returned to the main highway, going south, and looked for the next right turn to take us to the next bay which was Anchor Bay. These regions are pretty desolate but also very beautiful. At each stop, we got out and walked the rocky beach, took photographs and enjoyed the solitude.

Our next stop was at the triple bay area of Golden Bay, Ghajn Tuffieha Bay and Gnejna Bay. These three bays are next to each other, within walking distance and beautiful spaces to explore. This spot is quite different from the crowded and busy Sliema or even the not so crowded but fairly populated Mellieha Bay. This side of Malta also seems to have a large number of towers along the coast. I suppose that actually there are not any more than on the eastern side but it's just that here, they are more obvious because of the sparse area they inhabit. At one time, these towers served to warn the Maltese people of possible invaders. Going up and down the rocks that seem to be everywhere here did tire us a bit and made us hungry. We had been smart to pack a picnic lunch, basically the ever-famous Maltese bread, assorted cold cuts, olives, some fruit and the most important, cold beer. We were very content, relaxing on the rocks and enjoying the fantastic solitude and scenery. After our lunch break, relaxed and very tired, we made the decision to head back to our hotel in Mellieha. On the way, we did stop at the Kennedy Grove for a quick look. It's a park, southwest of St. Paul's Bay, where families go to relax and enjoy the outdoors. It consists of a round, columned memorial to our late president, John Kennedy, surrounded by parks. My children had been here with my parents on a visit quite some time ago and they told me about it. After that, we were ready for a possible nap and an afternoon at one of the pools at our hotel.

A late, quiet dinner, again in Mellieha, seemed appropriate and since we were tired, we chose to go to Rebekah's restaurant, which is lovely, charming, and close by. It also had the added attraction of a courtesy pick up and drop off from our hotel. Staff of the Radisson in St. Julian's on a previous trip had recommended it. Since we hadn't had the opportunity to try it before, we decided to try it now. We did not regret the choice. The restaurant, set in an old house with fairly large rooms, had great ambiance. The food was a bit pricey but it was really worth it. The rib eye was great; we both had it. After walking and climbing on the rocky western coast all day, it just hit the spot. Lingering on a few glasses of wine, we were ready to be driven back to our hotel and call it a day. Everyday seems to give us a new perspective on what is Malta. For such a small country, it does have diverse spots to visit depending on your mood.

Day 13 – Thursday, Valletta

Today we had a very different day. We did not drive all over Malta; we returned to one of the most important places, the Capital of Malta, Valletta. We had been there already but we had not seen it all yet!

Valletta was founded by a Grand Master and built on a grid pattern in 1566. It is the capital and serves as the island's center of social, cultural and economic activities. The whole town has been identified as a UNESCO World Heritage site and contains many interesting places to visit. It is certainly worth another visit and a whole day here.

We returned our rental on the outskirts of the city and continued on to Valletta by bus. Travel by bus is very easy. It was also fun because, as I mentioned earlier, I enjoyed listening to the Maltese language, especially when the participants did not know I understood them! Of course, we walked around the whole city, or, I should say, up and down the whole city. Many of the streets are structured as steps; it is that hilly here.

The first place we visited was St. John's Co-Cathedral. It is a most important and historical monument which was built by the Knights of St. John as their church in 1573. It also serves as a museum nowadays. I was asked to put on a skirt as I was wearing shorts. They seem to be prepared for this as they had a variety of skirts from which to choose. Within the Cathedral is the Oratory, which houses two of Caravaggio's paintings, the most important of which is his *The Beheading of St. John.* It is an unbelievably beautiful painting. Caravaggio had spent some time in Malta and these paintings are the result of that time. The Oratory was added in 1602. The Cathedral itself has ornately carved walls and the floors were inlaid with semi-precious stones.

Many of the side altars boasted marvelous paintings. As you look up, you notice that the ceilings, also, are embellished with art work. It is truly a museum! In addition, adjacent to the Cathedral, is a smaller museum which houses interesting exhibits of Flemish tapestries, church vestments and other interesting art objects. There were many other churches in Valletta, too numerous to list, too numerous to visit on a day plan but the Cathedral was definitely a must!

Another important building is the Grand Master's Palace. It was originally built as the official residence of the Grand Master of the Knights of St. John and later served as the residence of the British Governor. Today it serves as the Office of the President of Malta as well as the place where Parliament meets.

Fort St. Elmo, which we saw from the water in our harbor cruise and also visited earlier on our trip, is situated at the tip of Valletta and has defended the two harbors for centuries. Its most glorious moments can be documented in the Great Siege of 1565 as well as in World War II. Both of these historic events are well written about in books of their own.

Tired and hot, we were glad it was lunchtime because we had made plans to meet with my cousin Lydia again, to meet for lunch in Valletta.

We met at the planned meeting place, on the steps of the Cathedral and enjoyed another happy get together. We stopped for lunch in an open-air restaurant in the center of the city, the Republic Square, and had a very welcome lunch of pizza and beer. We relaxed and caught up on family news. Lydia had 11 brothers and sisters, presently strewn in the States and England, so we had a lot to talk about. It was good to get together with more family. It hasn't happened too often for us on this trip. It was a nice respite. As in all great squares, there are large numbers of pigeons, flying around, looking for bread and other foods, in Republic Square.

I imagine that the fact that the area is occupied by several outdoor restaurants helps a bit. However, I can still recall my mother telling me about visiting Republic Square (I think it had another name then) when I was a small child. It was, also, at that time, a nice place to stop and relax in the capital city although it did not yet have so many restaurants. However, at that time, I was nearly killed because, as a young child I was obsessed with chasing pigeons and did not see a Carrozzin, heading towards me. I was nearly run over by the horse pulling this method of transportation. I cried and cried and it took a lot of mommy comforting to make me feel good again. Being around four and seeing giant horse legs practically on me was very scary. At that time, Carozzins were a basic means of moving people as cars were not readily available or affordable in Malta in the Forties. Now they are simply a tourist method of transportation as are the horse and carriage in many other cities around the world.

Later, we thought it appropriate to start our afternoon with a visit to a show, which helps the visitor recapture the atmosphere, sounds and smells of The Great Siege. It's a thoroughly modern presentation using state of the art technology, videos and 3-D environments to showcase the historic Great Siege of 1565 when Malta was attacked by Saracens and in which the Knights of St. John emerged victorious. It was an exciting 45 minutes!

Another exciting show was The Malta Experience which we saw earlier. I mention it again because it is so worth seeing. In 45 minutes, the tourists are exposed to the entire 7000-year history of Malta, from the beginnings of the early settlers of the temple period to The Great Siege through the mass destruction in World War II. This show covers the turbulent history of the Maltese Islands, small islands buffeted by world events which continuously tested the bravery and resilience of the people. Highly recommended! Before we walked farther from the center of town, we visited another square, St. George's Square. Here we observed the changing of the guard outside the Grand Master's Palace. We also posed for photos by the British style mailboxes and phone booths that are still being used, though probably not for long. We stopped for a quick snack and sat for a while.

Now that we were well rested from traipsing back and forth on hilly streets and a quick walk through the center of town, we proceeded to go through some side streets to get to the Grand Harbor and to Upper Barrakka and more hills. It was quite a walk, uphill in the hot sun, on the edge of Valletta, but we were rewarded when we reached our destination. This was an area of attractive gardens, with palm trees and all sorts of flowering plants. Arches define the garden from the observation gallery where one has a stupendous view of Valletta's Grand Harbor and the surrounding fortified towns. We brought leftover food from lunch with us as we had been told that Upper Baracca has at least ten resident cats who are looking for snacks. They certainly enjoyed our leftover tidbits. Many cats inhabit the city and, I imagine, they keep the mouse population in control. With the other half, Lower Barrakka, these are beautiful gardens overlooking the harbor and each gives a different view, of one of the best harbors in the world. When we were having lunch, we had heard the cannons, which are shot here at noon by soldiers dressed in Victorian uniforms. This is truly one of the best views in Malta.

I remember visiting Upper Baracca a long time ago, as a young child. I had a photograph taken here at that time. It was interesting to note, as I had my photo with me this time, that practically nothing had changed in 50 years. The trees, statues and benches were still in the same place, just the trees were a bit larger, than they were right after the war.

It was now time to head back to our hotel because we had a dinner date with my cousin Diana. It was an easy trip as the bus terminal was just a walk out the main gate and quick to locate. The signs were very clear as to which bus to take.

Of course, we had plenty of time because in Malta, as in most of Europe, dinner is not served until at least 8 pm. We had time to get back to our hotel, relax, enjoy a cold drink and people watch for a while, and still have plenty of time to get ready to be picked up by Diana's son and enjoy another evening among relatives. Later, we got dressed and were ready to go when Carl and Joanna picked us up. Everyone here drives fast on very narrow roads and it seems that they have many close calls. Diana's house was similar to Liz's. Large areas of all the walls were covered with photographs and paintings. It seemed to be the style in Malta. All the tops of furniture were covered with collectibles and antiques. A lot of items to dust!

Dinner again was a banquet. We started out with a pasta course which I thought was meant to be the entrée. Wine flowed. After that, the entrée, beef bourguignon, potatoes, peas and corn, and of course, Maltese bread. A while later, we were offered a cheese platter with fruit and following, a delicious cake that Diana had baked.

With brief interludes for chatting, we were still eating after 11 pm. We had started around 8 pm. This eating large meals so late did not agree with my digestive system and we decided that tomorrow, we needed to take a break, eat less and much earlier than we had been doing.

Day 14 – Friday, Gozo

Today we planned to spend most of the day in Gozo. Unfortunately, it was still very hot here, as was the rest of the world. That made it very uncomfortable to walk around. But then, this was our big trip to Malta and we needed to make good use of our time here.

The first thing we did, after Joe picked us up, was to drive to the Ferry. One can take the bus or go on a shuttle but since we were already in Mellieha, close to the northern coast of Malta, it was a nice short drive. But then, of course, there was the long wait for the ferry to take us to Gozo (Ghawdex), just twenty minutes away.

Gozo is the second island that makes up the archipelago. In Greek mythology, it is the legendary home of Calypso, daughter of Atlas. It is inhabited, not as densely as Malta and it is considered a more relaxing place to visit. Many Maltese go to Gozo on vacation as there are some lovely resorts that are enjoyed by many.

Once we 'docked', Joe drove us around to get an idea of Gozo. Then he headed for the place I most wanted to visit, The Citadel. This is an impressive structure made up of battlements, a dramatic Cathedral and some quaint remains of old houses, many of which have been inhabited since the Bronze age. It seems to have been a fortification of sorts high up on a hill overlooking all Gozo. As a result, this whole group of buildings, sitting on a rocky cliff had superior views of the whole island. It had existed since Roman times but the current structure is fairly 'new', just since the 17th century. The Citadel, as many important places in Malta, is included in the list of tentative UNESCO World Heritage sites since 1998.

It is a combination of medieval castle and an early modern fortress. It was quite a feat climbing all the steps to The Citadel, especially in the heat. We spent some time in the Cathedral which, we were told, was built over the place that was originally a temple dedicated to Juno. We entered the Baroque Roman Catholic Cathedral of the Assumption built in 1697 and marveled at its size. We also visited the Archaeological Museum which focused on the History of Gozo starting with pre-historic times and ending with the medieval periods.

It is hard to imagine the real, original structure as it was now under construction. They are renovating the fortress to make it more user friendly for the tourists. (Maybe they'll even install an elevator?) Many visitors were unable to climb up the steps to see the view and the Cathedral at the top of the fortress. In fact, the two men in our party chose to wait for us in the car while we three ladies, Liz, Diana and I, trudged up to see the specific buildings.

While we were still exploring, we were fortunate to hear the bronze cannon being fired at noon making a sound that could be heard over all the valley below.

Because Bob and Joe had chosen to wait for us, parked down the hill, they were a bit upset that we took over an hour looking at the site. We could have taken longer, it was that interesting. We did meet a couple who managed the climb, took our photograph and chatted with us for a while. It was a marvelous experience!

Later, as Liz, Diana and I got back to the car, Joe took us to several places. One, specifically was a 'land bridge' which had many, many tourists and plenty of scuba divers. It was called The Azure Window and I am so glad to have seen it as a year later it succumbed to a wild storm, which tore it and plunged it into the Mediterranean. This famous tourist attraction, a ninety-two-foot-high limestone arch that had been eroding for some time, was even featured in the premier of *Game of Thrones*.

After enjoying the view, we stopped for a cold beer. We also visited the Alabaster Caves – caves with colorful alabaster stalactites and stalagmites that were very unique to explore. We made a quick visit to

Ggantija Prehistoric Temples in Xaghra and then continued on to see the Fungus Rock and the Inland Sea. Considering we only allotted one day to visit Gozo, we tried to cover more places than we really could. We did however manage a quick visit to the Craft Village, a former military base turned into a local handicrafts center. Again, beautiful handmade ceramics, glass pieces, Maltese lace and the most famous Filigree Maltese Crosses in either gold or silver were the popular items sold here.

We also managed to visit Xlendi, a landlocked sandy and pebbly beach, tucked away under towering cliffs, beautiful to see. And lastly, we visited Calypso's Cave situated on a cliff's edge. According to tradition this cave was supposedly the place where Homer's Ulysses lived for years with the nymph Calypso. The cliff itself overlooks Ramla l'Hamra, a sandy beach that takes its name from the reddish color of the sand there.

Not having had enough, we drove around a bit more, trying to see as much as we could in the time allowed. We finally settled in another small fishing village, Marsalforn, where we enjoyed a very late lunch, outdoors in the beautiful seacoast of Gozo.

These excursions were planned by Joe to give us a complete and total view of Malta and Gozo but sometimes I felt like we took in too much. Yes, it was not a 'rest' vacation. We were going just about every minute but the final result was that we saw a great deal more than most tourists see in 15 days and we have photographs and memories that will last us for more than a lifetime. After more sightseeing, from the car, we again headed for the Ferry and by late afternoon we were back in our hotel. We did enjoy a brief swim in the pool but we were quite a bit tired and never even went out for dinner as we were still full after our late lunch. Later, from our balcony, we could see the local church, all decked out in lights for another Festa coming up that weekend.

Day 15 – Saturday, Paceville

Well, we felt really good. We had covered everything that was on our schedule and we still had a whole day to relax and enjoy Malta as tourists.

We planned on going to the beach at our previous hotel in Sliema to enjoy our day by the pool and sunbathe on the rocks nearby. It was nice of the hotel management to allow us to use the pool even though we were no longer guests. We brought reading materials and planned to just do nothing for a full day.

The Mediterranean water felt great, cool and refreshing and, I must admit, using the pool instead of swimming off the rocks was much more comfortable. Rocks can be slippery and, since I'm not a swimmer, the pool was a lot safer.

For lunch, we again enjoyed the offerings of the Tiki Hut. Cool drinks, and nice large hamburgers and fries filled the bill. And after lunch we took the bus to our hotel in Mellieha, to unwind, relax in air-conditioned comfort and pack.

Tonight, since we had time, we decided, to explore Paceville. This was not originally scheduled on this vacation but, after all, we had not danced for two whole weeks, we had some free time, so we decided to go. We did not go to dinner, as we knew that we would snack our way through the nightlife capital of Malta.

For this trip, we chose to take a taxi. It was much more convenient than a bus and busses do stop running at a certain time of the night. Also, we wanted to go on our own for a nice relaxing evening with no specific scheduled time to return to our hotel. It turned out to be a good idea because even though we did not stay until the wee hours typical of Paceville, we did stay later than usual for us.

Paceville is an exciting town covered with nightclubs, bars, discos, cinemas and much more. It includes the Sky Club, one of the largest clubs in Malta, one that is used for concerts and large group gatherings throughout the year. Of the many clubs, we chose Plush, just about the most popular, as it was located at the corner of a busy pedestrian intersection, easy to find, hard to miss. As we got to Paceville quite a while before the young crowds populated the area, it was not yet as busy as it would be later in the evening.

Plush has indoor and outdoor seating areas, with couches for comfort, and we sat outside for a while and had drinks and snacks. Later, we went to the Plush Lounge, upstairs, with its famous red and black lighting, and spent a nice amount of time dancing to the latest hits. It still amazed me that here, in the small island of Malta, they were just as up to date with their music as any club in the states.

Other clubs in Paceville included BarCelone Lounge, Havana, Shadow Lounge, Smooth and Jazz as well as probably others we had not seen.

Again, for my idea of Malta, it was a hopping place!

We enjoyed ourselves tremendously simply because we were not even expecting to be there but it did get late and we did have to fly out the next morning. Fortunately, after all the dancing we did, we knew we would be sitting on a plane for hours tomorrow. Calling a taxi again was the simplest and safest way to get to our hotel and we got there quickly. If you're a regular driver, in Malta, everything is close and driving is fast.

So, we did get to Paceville on this trip after all and had a wonderful time. Just one more memory to add to the many we've collected. This was a good trip by any definition.

Day 16 – Sunday, Going home

We were picked up at 9:15 by our cousin Joe, his wife, Liz and her sister, Diana and taken to Hal Luqa Airport where we started our trip back home. Amid lots of hugs and kisses and promises to 'come back soon' we tearfully said our good-byes. As always, I leave Malta sad and happy. Sad to be leaving my family and the land of my birth, happy to be returning to my adopted country, the United States, which has been my home for many more years than Malta had been and where I met my husband, had my wonderful children and, most likely where I will live for the rest of my life.

Thank You for Reading Return to Melita

Please post a review on Amazon.com

Visit my blog to see many of the places mentioned

in this book come to life in beautiful color.

annevisitsmalta.com

La Maison Publishing, Inc.
Vero Beach Florida
The Hibiscus City
lamaisonpublishing@gmail.com

CPSIA information can be obtained
at www.ICGtesting.com
Printed in the USA
LVHW032323250219
608762LV00001B/59